A Land

ORDINARY

in Business and Ministry:

PEOPLE

How They Lead,

EXTRAORDINARY

Where They Stumble,

LEADERS

What Helps Them Succeed

Foreword by
JOHN MULFORD, Ph.D.
DEAN, REGENT UNIVERSITY GRADUATE SCHOOL OF BUSINESS

A Landmark Study of Christians

ORDINARY

in Business and Ministry:

PEOPLE

How They Lead,

EXTRAORDINARY

Where They Stumble,

LEADERS

What Helps Them Succeed

MICHAEL A. ZIGARELLI, Ph.D.
REGENT UNIVERSITY GRADUATE SCHOOL OF BUSINESS

ƧYNERGY Publishers
Gainesville, Florida 32614 USA

A division of Bridge-Logos International Trust
in partnership with **Bridge-Logos** *Publishers*

Ordinary People, Extraordinary Leaders
by Michael A. Zigarelli, Ph.D.
© 2002 by Michael A. Zigarelli. All rights reserved

International Standard Book Number: 1-931727-07-4
Library of Congress Catalog Card Number: 2002104226

Published by:
Synergy Publishers
Gainesville, Florida 32614 USA
www.synergypublishers.com

Synergy Publishers is a division of Bridge-Logos International Trust, Inc., a not-for-profit corporation, in partnership with Bridge-Logos Publishers.

DEDICATION

Humbly and gratefully dedicated to the One who has had His hand on this project from its inception. May many be as blessed in reading this book as its author has been in writing it.

CONTENTS

FOREWORD

How do Christians approach their jobs? Do they have an explicitly Christian framework and principles for their work? Or, perhaps they haven't consciously thought about how their Christianity affects their work life, even though they could tell you the values they would like their lives to reflect.

Regent University Graduate School of Business (RGSB) has been teaching biblical principles of business for twenty years, but the teachers had only anecdotal information about how those principles are actually working in business. Mike Zigarelli, who joined the RGSB faculty in 1999, was not content to teach how Christians ought to behave without also discovering how they actually behave in the workplace.

What if there is a disconnect? What if people either don't know how they should behave or they are defeated in achieving the behavior they want by internal or external obstacles? Dr. Zigarelli reasoned that if we knew how Christians were approaching their work and what they perceived to be the problems in living out their faith, we might develop tools that would help them achieve their goals.

Most students of the Bible could list the values that it teaches—do unto others as you would have them do unto you, have compassion and mercy on people as God does, tell the truth, keep your promises, don't steal, don't envy or covet, don't be prideful, be a good steward of the resources in your care, etc. But even though most could agree on these statements of principle, they might see them differently in action in today's business environment.

How do people of faith grapple with the challenges of daily life in the marketplace? Do they order their principles from most to least important? How do they decide which principles apply in a given situation? Do they always do what their values indicate or do they sometimes know the right thing but do something else? If so, why?

For example, in downsizing, a manager might be told to reduce his staff by a certain number or percentage. Who should go and who should stay? Should he choose by seniority, because that is the fair thing to do? Should he keep those who have the most need for the job, because that is the compassionate thing to do? Should he keep the top performers because that is the best stewardship decision? Should he keep his best friends because they will be loyal to him? A list of agreed upon principles doesn't seem to do the job if you don't know how to apply them.

Dr. Zigarelli's book gives us an unusual look into values in action—how people think and behave in real life. These people aren't hypothetical analytical machines who can always apply their values rationally even in emotionally charged situations. They are flesh and blood human beings who sometimes do heroic deeds, sometimes shrink from the right choice out of fear and sometimes stumble along because their thinking is fuzzy.

This book is a marvelous first step in what should be a rich study of Christians in the marketplace. Its findings are very encouraging. People who are deeply committed to Jesus Christ, are also deeply committed to following His ways.

The one attribute of Christ that comes out most clearly in His followers is their commitment to people, especially those they supervise. Things that seem ordinary—such as taking an interest in someone's life and professional development—done by ordinary people with faults and weaknesses, produce extraordinary results.

The fact that ordinary people can be extraordinary leaders by practicing a small set of basic principles may surprise many readers. Yet it is entirely consistent with the findings of a study that focuses on highly successful leaders. In his book, *Good to Great*, Jim Collins states that the CEO in every company he identified as going from good to great exhibited a paradox of humility and strong professional will. These leaders cared about people and gave them credit for the organization's success.

But knowing the secret to success, doesn't guarantee success for everyone. How many have made weight loss a New Year's resolution and failed to stay with the program to achieve it? Even though we know what to do—eat less and exercise—and we know what the result will be—many of us can't seem to achieve our goal.

Dr. Zigarelli goes beyond identifying best practices of Christian principles in business to identifying obstacles to living out those best practices. This book is a foundational, seminal work to what I believe will be an amazingly productive vein of research with tremendous practical application.

Dr. Zigarelli's ongoing work in Christian formation, character development, and behavior in the workplace should provide biblically sound tools that have proven themselves in peoples' lives in the marketplace. They won't be magic bullets. Without discipline—spiritual diet and exercise—no one will become an extraordinary leader. But when people understand the mechanism by which their actions produce good results and they see examples of ordinary people who have become extraordinary leaders, they will be more likely to practice the disciplines that lead to such success.

John Mulford, Ph.D.
Dean
Regent University
Graduate School of Business

ACKNOWLEDGMENTS

People around Regent University and around the world greatly enhanced the quality of this book by lending their time, their encouragement and their professional expertise. The faculty of the Regent University Graduate School of Business assisted in the creation and fine-tuning of the survey instrument, as well as in the interpretation of the results and in the editing of the book. My thanks in this regard go out to Dean John Mulford and to Professors Ken Burger, Randy Case, Dan Chamberlin, Dail Fields, Ralph Miller, Tim Redmer, Greg Stone, and Diane Wiater, and to Professor Bruce Winston of the Center for Leadership Studies.

I'm similarly grateful to the Regent M.B.A. and Ph.D. students who seemed to enlist in this project at just the right time, contributing exactly what was needed for the critical task of survey administration. Special thanks here to Luke Nichter, Robbin Coffey, Diane Ross and Jacque King. I am also indebted to the good folks at Synergy Publishers, especially to Dennis Watson and Marianne Graves, whose editorial acumen considerably improved the final product.

Lastly, but in many ways most importantly, a word of appreciation to the many "ordinary people" who invested their valuable time to complete a detailed survey about their priorities and practices at work. Without you, this work certainly would not be possible. It is my hope and prayer that generations of values-centered leaders and managers will benefit from the information and insights that you have so generously provided.

INTRODUCTION

If you're like many of the people I expect to read this book, you've read other leadership resources. You've probably read books about Christian leaders and managers and how they live their faith in the workplace. You've perhaps heard a sermon or two on the topic. You may have even taken—or led—a seminar on leadership or gone to a Christian school where they teach such subjects. I've done all those things too and as I did, I became increasingly dissatisfied with what I was receiving.

It's not that what's available isn't useful. It has *tremendous* value and collectively, these resources have taught millions, including me, about the principles and practices of Christian-based leadership.

The problem I began to have with the literature and teaching in this genre was this: the information was less encompassing than I would have liked it to be. What I mean is that I found no "big picture" from which I could learn. There was no large-scale study that tapped the experiences of seasoned Christian leaders.[1]

Instead, most of the Christian leadership resources approach the subject anecdotally, telling the story of an organization or of a group of leaders. Others are primarily exegetical, culling leadership principles straight from scripture and applying them in contemporary context. Some are biographical, using the life of a Biblical figure as normative for our day. Some, unfortunately, amount to mere musings from some guy with a word processor and a publishing contract.

Priorities, Practices and Challenges

You may have asked the same question that kept coming up in my mind: "What do Christians actually *do* as leaders and what, if anything, can we learn from their experiences?" I had read about what they were supposed to be doing as people of faith, and I had read about the practices of a handful of them in these books, but nothing revealed the priorities, practices and challenges of Christians generally. So I looked into it myself. This book—a study of over 300 Christian leaders in various work environments—is the product of that endeavor and it fills some of the gap in this literature.

I should say up front, though, that exposure to those other books is not a requirement for the fruitful use of this book. For this class in Christian leadership, there are no prerequisites. *Ordinary People, Extraordinary Leaders* doesn't directly build on the ideas articulated elsewhere. Rather, it's intended to be a fresh look at Christian leadership using sound quantitative and qualitative research methods

Overview of My Approach & My Leaders' Survey

Let me be clear about one thing: this study is a not a look at *all* Christians in the workplace. Instead, *it's a look at those Christians who desire to put their faith into practice in the workplace* (unfortunately, there is a difference). Please bear with me if I remind you of this point too often in this book. I simply do not want to risk misrepresenting the findings or having them misinterpreted. This is a study of Christians who take their faith seriously and aspire to live that faith outside of their church walls, and in particular, in their places of employment.

I've included an appendix in this book to describe the full methodology for those who want more information on such points. For now, suffice it to say that I identified my respondents by their affiliation in Christian management and leadership associations or by their participation in an intentionally Christian business school program. I collected a wealth of information from 328 leaders across 31 states and supplemental information about the obstacles to Christian leadership from an additional 124 leaders.

The Demographics

Demographically, this is a sundry sample. Most (63%) work in the for-profit sector, with the balance employed in churches, charities, camps, pregnancy centers, the military, schools, law enforcement, and federal, state and local government. Similar to the population of interest here, the majority of the sample is male (73%) and white (83%). They average about 45 years of age and 15 years of management experience. More than half (59%) are in top management positions (VP or higher). On average, they have been Christian for 27.5 years and they represent 28 denominations.

A diverse group, indeed, with diverse experiences and, to some extent, diverse opinions. It is my hope that through exposure to these leaders' varied insights:

- You will glean helpful ideas about implementation of your faith at work.
- You will be encouraged and motivated by the successes of other Christian leaders.
- You will be liberated by the knowledge that others don't do it perfectly either.

- You will see more clearly the obstacles to applying your faith at work.
- You will identify means by which you can address and eventually overcome those obstacles.

Warning: We've Discarded the Rose-Colored Glasses

Before moving into the content of the book, please note one more thing. This book does not adopt the presupposition that because one is a committed Christian, one is an exemplary leader. Far from it, as we know from our exposure to Christians who fall well short of the ideal (They are, after all, merely mortal).

Through this research, I have identified some Christians who, by their own admission, do not care very much about their employees, who have little desire to serve customers well, who are not very approachable, who are impatient, harsh, joyless, and self-centered and some who—again by their own admission—are not terribly efficient or effective in achieving results.

I report such findings because I am not playing ostrich. This book is not about highlighting the merits of Christian leaders and disregarding their faults and weaknesses. Nor is it about disproportionately emphasizing where Christians fall short in leadership. Rather, this book is about "what is"—the negatives, the positives and the pathways from the former to the latter.

Accordingly, the content, in large part, is descriptive. It provides an overview, for the first time, of Christian leaders' priorities, practices and challenges in the workplace. Some of the content, though (namely chapters 6 through 8), is prescriptive. I share what I've learned about how to bridge the gap between what is and what should be for the Christian.

So in the interest of full disclosure, let me say that if you're looking for agendas in this book, you'll find two:
(1) To profile objectively the committed Christian leader and
(2) To help Christians learn from the collective experience and wisdom of other Christians

This approach is not very controversial, I know, and it might not sell a million copies, but it's my hope that this resource will achieve a more transcendent objective: equipping you to more effectively lead people and organizations—to become an "extraordinary leader"—by letting God lead you.

Notes

1. One notable exception here is Laura Nash's *Believers in Business* (Thomas Nelson, 1994), an excellent study of seventy-five Christian CEOs.

CHAPTER 1

EMPLOYEE MANAGEMENT

WASHING EMPLOYEES' FEET WITHOUT THROWING IN THE TOWEL ON RESULTS

Several decades ago, researchers Robert Blake and Jane Mouton introduced the world to a path-breaking conceptualization of effective management called "The Managerial Grid." The grid is simple. It's essentially two axes, one representing a manager's concern for people and the other representing the manager's concern for production (see Figure 1-1).

Although there are many management styles represented on the grid (e.g., high concern for people, little concern for production; high concern for production, little concern for people), as you might guess, the "ideal manager" is the one who is high on both dimensions.

It's not rocket science, but in the 1960s, it was an important contribution to help organizations and individual managers understand what they should be striving for on a daily basis. It still is. In the years since

1

Figure 1-1
The Managerial Grid

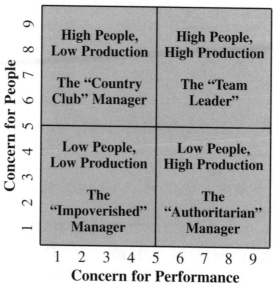

the grid's introduction, it has become a pillar of management theory, providing a framework for what leaders' priorities should be.

Interestingly, when examining the priorities and practices of the Christian leaders I surveyed, a profile emerged that looks very much like that of the ideal manager from the grid. Looking first at the "concern for people" dimension, it is clear that Christian leaders genuinely do care about their employees. Employee needs matter to them—a lot.

In fact, as shown in Figure 1-2, when these leaders were asked to rank the importance of various stakeholder needs, employee needs ranked second, behind customer needs but ahead of the needs of one's boss, the shareholders,[1] the local community, suppliers and

Figure 1-2
Which Stakeholder Needs Are Most Important?

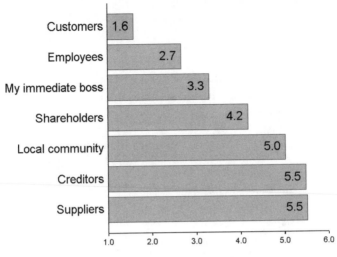

Average Ranking of Importance (1 to 7)

creditors. In fact, almost one in five leaders (17%) put employee needs *at the very top* of this stakeholder list.

Now, seventeen percent first place votes may seem like a trivial number to some (why isn't it two in five or three in five if Christians are to be servant-leaders?), but recognize that we work in a world where customers and shareholders are traditionally considered paramount. A second place overall ranking for employees, coupled with a significant proportion of first place votes bears testimony to the fact that Christian leaders are indeed highly employee-oriented, relative to the culture in which they work.

> *Leaders take care of their employees, employees take care of the customers, and the customers return more often to the organization.*
>
> Steve Ledbetter
> Major
> Fayetteville Police Dept.
> Georgia

3

We found other evidence to confirm this conclusion. Consider these striking statistics. More than four out of five leaders moderately or strongly agree that:

- It's their job to develop their employees' careers (84%)
- It's their job to resolve conflict among their employees quickly (83%)
- It's their job to reduce the work-related stress of employees (82%)

Sounds like the type of people for whom you'd like to work, doesn't it? Employee needs are a priority for them, from basics like a low-stress, low-conflict work environment to higher-level needs like career growth and development.

I try not to see myself as 'above' my employees. This helps me to keep God's perspective.

Bryan Makus
Network Engineer
Automatic Data Processing
New Jersey

A separate survey question makes this point even clearer. A majority of these leaders (55%) say they "strongly agree" with the statement, "It is a high priority for me to serve the needs of my employees," and another 33% report "moderate" agreement with this statement. All told, that's about nine out of ten (88%) saying that service to their employees is a "high priority." Beyond this, as we'll explore in more detail in this chapter, Christian leaders are very accessible to their employees. They regularly solicit employee input and many have made a habit of encouraging and praising those they lead. Unless they are stretching the truth on this survey (something they really have no incentive to do), committed Christians are not your run-of-the-mill bosses. They really care about the people they lead in the workplace.

There's another side to this love story, though. These leaders are sensitive to employee needs, but they are not "hyper-sensitive." For the most part, although meeting employee needs is a high priority, it does

Whether it's getting them what they need to do their job or addressing distractions like power plays and conflict, I see my role as making the way clear for them to do their jobs.

Terri Swetnem
CFO
American Psychiatric Association
Virginia

not completely dominate their thinking. They're not managers who neglect production concerns. Actually, the contrary is true. Their concern for production—for performance and results—is at least as high, if not higher, than their concern for people. Employee needs do matter, and they matter a lot, but not usually at the expense of broader organizational needs. How do we know? As shown in this chapter, when there is tension between employee concerns and organizational performance concerns, the latter often win out. We'll see this primacy of performance when we look at Christian leaders' criteria for giving a raise and at their resistance to weighing employee family need in their decision-making.

So the big picture looks like this: the profile of the Christian leader is one of high people-orientation and high results-orientation. They are sensitive and even loving to employees, but they will sometimes subordinate that individual care when it potentially inhibits organizational performance. Let's now look more closely at these practices.

CEOs ("Chief Encouragement Officers," that is)

Throughout scripture, Christians are called to be encouragers of those around them (see, for example, 1 Thessalonians 5:11, Proverbs 15:23, Proverbs 31:31). In the context of the workplace, this means that it is the responsibility of the Christian leader to recognize and praise employees for their efforts—to pat them on the back for a job well done, to commend and publicize their successes and to actively support their continued effort on behalf of the organization.

Employee recognition is also a practice that comports with contemporary business thinking about human relations. Acclaimed as more than just a nice or ethical thing to do, encouragement and public praise have been touted in recent years as vehicles to greater employee satisfaction, productivity

> Do little things that are not expensive but show Christ's love, like birthday cards for employees and their families and gift certificates for exceptional performance.
>
> Kevin DeWeese
> President
> Level Ride Manufacturing
> Missouri

and retention. So at least two good reasons exist for Christian leaders to become Chief Encouragement Officers—one scriptural and one financial. It is a practice that resides squarely in the intersection of serving employees and maximizing performance.

Accordingly, I asked the question: "How often would you say that you deliver some sort of praise to an employee?"[2] The average response was halfway between "once a week" and "every few days"—call it about every three or four days. Not bad in a culture where we too often

6

tend to keep our compliments to ourselves, but there's room for improvement.

I try to tell people in my organization what I really value in them, and when I introduce them to someone, I extol their best traits.

Barry Pollara
Senior Vice President
Paine Webber
Virginia

Looking closer at those who have really made this a habit (those who say they praise employees daily), we see that more than one in three leaders (35%) claim to praise employees every day. Interestingly, a preponderance of these "CEOs" are female. Fifty percent of the women surveyed as compared to fewer than one-third of the men (31.5%) report delivering praise daily.

The good news for men is that to make praising employees a habit, they don't need costly surgery to change genders. Instead, there

Being filled with the Spirit fills your heart with love and compassion for all.

Anonymous Respondent
Texas

is another pathway to becoming a more encouraging manager. As shown in Figure 1-3, there is a connection between Christian maturity and the practice of praising

Figure 1-3
The Habit of Praise Begins with Maturity

Christian Maturity
- More prayer
- More Scripture-reading
- More dependence on God

⇨ Greater love and concern for employees ⇨ Habitual practice of praising employees

employees. Compared to other leaders I studied, the encouragers in this sample appear to pray more, to read scripture more and to be more dependent on God. And interestingly, the critical link between Christian maturity and employee praise appears to be straight from a management textbook: "concern for people." Greater God-centeredness in a leader is strongly correlated with greater love for one's employees and that greater love leads to more generous praise and encouragement of those employees.

There's more news too: an encouragement—performance linkage exists. Those who praise employees frequently are more likely to report being able to *get results*. I would conjecture that there is a causal relationship here. Encouragement of employees inspires them to both loyalty and commitment, a tandem that facilitates a leader's ability to get results. Recognizing and praising employees is one of those "best practices" of leaders who are concerned for people *and* concerned about performance.

Many Christian Leaders Are Approachable

Approaching the Boss

Overall, Christian leaders claim to be reasonably accessible to their employees. On average, they "moderately agree" with the statement: "My employees would say that they can talk to me about almost anything," and almost four in ten (37%) "strongly agree."

As with praising employees, female leaders tend to be a little better at this than are men. As indicated in Figure 1-4, more than half of the female respondents "strongly agree" that their employees can talk to them

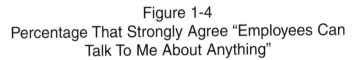

Figure 1-4
Percentage That Strongly Agree "Employees Can Talk To Me About Anything"

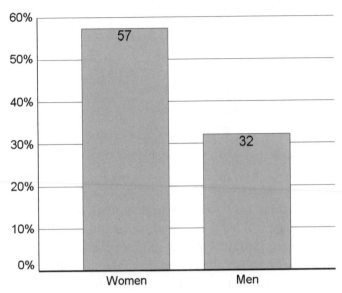

about anything, whereas only about one-third of the male respondents "strongly agree."

Why would women leaders be more approachable than are men? Is it because women are in lower level leadership positions and perhaps less busy? Is it because they have fewer people reporting to them and can spend more time with each subordinate? Do their fewer years of management experience somehow explain their greater accessibility?

Actually, none of these differences explains the gender gap here. What does explain it is *women's greater level of care for those around them in the workplace.* Similar to the findings above regarding employee praise, I found that women's higher self-reported levels of "love," "kindness" and "generosity" at work primarily account for the differences in approachability.[3]

It is so important to be real and approachable. While some managers would like to keep a respectful distance, I find that accessibility is the key to showcasing your faith.

Cynthia Thomas
Front Desk Manager
Sport & Health Club
Virginia

That stands to reason. Employees are more likely to believe that they can talk to a manager candidly when they perceive that this manager actually cares about them. Accordingly, Christian leaders who desire to be more accessible to their followers may need to do more than implement an "open-door policy." What's required, it seems, is more of an "open-heart policy," feeling and expressing a genuine concern for those they lead. As noted above, and as explained further in chapter 8, greater Christian maturity—greater God-centeredness—may be the primary pathway to such concern.

Approaching the Employees

The proverb is credited to King Solomon: "Plans fail for lack of counsel, but with many advisors, they succeed" (Proverbs 15:22). There is wisdom in seeking and taking advice from people. There is prideful folly in the assumption that we have all the answers and cannot learn anything from others.

I asked about the extent to which leaders solicit input from their employees and by and large, it appears that Christian

I don't have all the right answers. In all non-emergencies, I encourage my men to question me.

Grayson McClain
Submarine Communications Officer
U.S. Navy

leaders have adopted Solomon's advice. Forty percent claim to seek employee input on a daily basis for decision-making and about seven out of ten (69%) say they seek input "every day" or "every few days." There are no differences here by gender, by number of direct reports, by years of management experience or by the position held by the leader (see Figure 1-5).

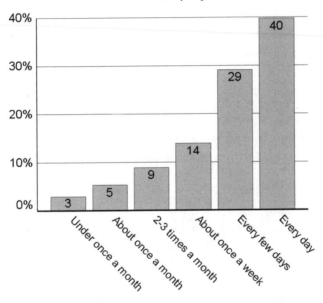

Figure 1-5
How Often Do You Seek Input
From Your Employees?

Want a Raise? Get Results (or at least try hard)

What's relevant when the Christian leader gives a raise? What's considered most important? Leaders were asked to rank the following five criteria for giving a raise (with "1" being the highest criterion): the employee's performance, the effort of the employee, the family need of the employee, retention of the employee and the inflation rate. Figure 1-6 summarizes the results.

Like many of their secular counterparts, Christian leaders accord the greatest weight to the employee's performance. A whopping 75% ranked performance the number one consideration, with another 22% ranking it second.

Looking closer, women were slightly more likely to rank performance first than were men (80 to 74 percent). Otherwise, there were no differences based on job level, years of managerial experience or employment in a for-profit versus not-for-profit organization.

Figure 1-6
What's Most Important When Giving A Raise?

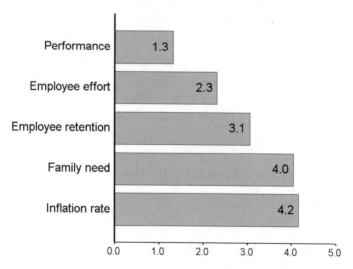

Average Ranking of Importance (1 to 5)

Lest we think that Christian leaders might be too performance-minded when rewarding employees, though, note that "employee effort" ranks a clear second among the five pay raise criteria. Apparently, trying hard really counts if you ask Christian leaders. It's not just results that matter. Many Christian leaders reward, in part, based on how hard their employees are working.

In fact, almost one in five (18.8%) of these leaders ranks employee effort *ahead* of performance. Moreover, few seem to devalue the effort criterion: a mere one in ten (9.9%) ranks effort fourth or fifth among the five pay raise criteria.[4]

> *Pay people fairly. Encourage people often. Confront people in private.*
>
> Ron Brown
> Ministry Coordinator
> Youth for Christ
> Illinois

Rounding out our examination of Figure 1-6, "employee retention" ranks third when giving a raise, ahead of family need and the inflation rate, which are statistically tied for last place. We'll explore next this result regarding the low priority of employee family need.

When Performance Conflicts with Family Needs

Nowhere is the tension between concern for employees and concern for production more evident than it is in situations involving family need. How sensitive are Christian leaders to employee family needs when giving a pay raise or making a hiring decision? Does family need trump performance and qualifications when leaders make such critical managerial decisions?

No, it often doesn't matter. The responses in these two areas, detailed next, reveal an important story: *Christian*

13

leaders are resistant to making decisions based on employee family needs and they resist because of performance concerns.

Pay Raises

We saw that family needs tied for last among the pay raise criteria. It's just not that important when compared to the more traditional determinates of pay. We'll see why in a moment.

Hiring

For the related hiring question, leaders were asked to what extent they agree or disagree with the following statement: "It is appropriate to hire someone who *is not* the most qualified applicant

> *I used to hire the applicant with slightly less talent but more need. This act of benevolence almost always proved to be a mistake.*
>
> Charles Rutherford
> CEO
> Mobile One Corporation
> Minnesota

for a job if that person needs the job more than the other applicants." Consistent with their responses to the pay raise question, Christian leaders *disagree* that it is appropriate to hire a less qualified applicant who has greater need for the job. There wasn't a lot of variance here either: 52% strongly disagree and another 22% moderately disagree. Fewer than one in five (18%) express any level of agreement at all (mild to strong) with the appropriateness of letting a person's need for the job drive a hiring decision.

Now, these findings would not be news if I were sampling freshly-minted Harvard Business School grads. But these are over 300 committed Christians I'm talking about here. Ninety-eight percent of them strongly agree with the statements: "I believe in the divinity of Jesus Christ" and "I have made a personal commitment to Jesus Christ that is still important in my life today." Moreover, they overwhelmingly affirm that: "At work, I consider God to be my ultimate boss." This is as close to a workplace "What Would Jesus Do?" (WWJD) crowd as we can get. So why doesn't the belief in workplace WWJD translate into significantly weighing family need in managerial decision-making?

To examine this, I looked more closely at the folks who had the *least sensitivity* to family need—quite a large sample, in fact (n=134). What's different about this group that might account for their attitudes in hiring and compensation? What explains why they resist considering family need in decision-making? The answer is that they have an uncompromising focus on performance.

Personal concerns of the employee are our concerns too.

Herrick Garnsey
CEO
Garnsey & Wheeler Ford
Colorado

Without getting into too many technical details of the analysis, the responses to the hiring question show that Christian leaders who "strongly disagree" with considering applicant personal need in hiring were also the people who: (1) most highly value performance appraisal systems and (2) determine raises based primarily on employee performance. In other words, they are performance-driven leaders. Moreover, looking at the pay raise data, those who rank family need dead last on the compensation question are more likely to believe the traditional business axiom that *profit is an end rather than a means.*[5] A logical conclusion from these results is that the Christian leaders who tend to be insensitive to employee family need are insensitive because employee performance and financial performance govern their decisions. Performance is king of their decision-making hill.

By all means, 'noblesse oblige.' Act kindly toward those under you whether they can benefit you or not!

Lynda Ghaedi
Owner
20th Century Realty
Florida

But interestingly, God is allegedly atop that hill too. This same group agrees just as strongly as everyone else that: "God is my ultimate boss." Is this a tension, and if so, what are we to make of it?

After teaching Christian leaders for a number of years, I would speculate—and I emphasize *speculate*—that there is a tension in some Christians' approach to leadership and management, but many Christians are not even aware of it. They affirm love and mercy, generosity and servanthood, but at the same time, they make performance a higher priority. Whether they do so on the grounds of "business reality" or financial stewardship (chapter 2), the fact remains that for many Christian leaders in the workplace, performance is a dominant virtue and as such, it drives pay and hiring decisions.

None of this is to say, of course, that Christians should be unconcerned or even less concerned about employee performance or organizational performance. Running a business, ministry or work group to the glory of God *demands* the pursuit of excellence and top performance. In doing so, though, Christians need to be wary of the potential for performance orientation to become an idol, crowding out a true "concern for people"—true Christlike compassion for those God has entrusted to them in the workplace.

Notes

1. The shareholder needs ranking remained the same when we looked strictly at respondents in the for-profit sector. However, it is not known which of these respondents are employed in publicly held companies. My conjecture is that if one looked only at organizations that have shareholders, those needs might be ranked somewhat higher than fourth place.
2. The complete item endeavors to be more balanced, reading: "Some people make it a high priority to praise their employees for their efforts and achievements. Others do not, sometimes because they do not consider praise to be a useful business practice, sometimes because they are too overworked to spend time praising employees. About how often would you say you deliver some sort of praise to an employee?"
3. This conclusion is based on a regression model that included job level, managerial experience, number of direct reports and the self-reported virtue variables of love, kindness and generosity.
4. I found no differences here based on gender, years of experience, job level, employment in the for-profit sector or number of years as a Christian.
5. The specific survey item reads as follows: "Profit is a means, not an end" (strongly disagree to strongly agree). We'll see in chapter 2 that conceptualizing profit as an end is, in fact, a counter-Biblical perspective.

CHAPTER 2

FINANCIAL STEWARDSHIP

CHRISTIAN LEADERS SERVE
THE BETTER MASTER

Some Context for the Survey Questions & Results

Because some may not be familiar with the concept of "stewardship"—a concept that is central to this chapter—let's begin with some context for our discussion.

The Bible teaches that Christians are to act as *stewards*, not owners, of the financial resources at their disposal. In a workplace setting, this would mean that they are to be stewards of their budget, stewards of the firm's profits, stewards of charitable contributions, stewards of the congregation's tithes and so on. Moreover, the concept extends beyond money. Christians are also to be stewards of the personal blessings God has conferred upon them. At work, this would mean using gifts like one's talents, one's time and one's position of authority for God's purposes.

This pervasive Biblical principle derives from both the Old and New Testament teaching that everything—including money—belongs to God and that people are to manage (i.e., steward) those God-owned resources in accordance with God's will.[1] I should clarify from the outset, though, that this theology of stewardship does not hold that money is evil, that making money is somehow "wrong" or that it is a "sin" to pursue profit. Far from it. It's not the money *per se* that's the problem or even the active pursuit of money that's the problem. As made clear in the Epistles, the "love of money"—the idolization of money—is the problem (1 Timothy 6:10). To put this in practical terms, Christians are admonished to avoid putting financial concerns ahead of God's concerns when making decisions. Money and profit are not to be conceptualized as ends in themselves, but as a means to greater, God-honoring ends. The gifts, talents and positions conferred by God are to be used in the same way.

In light of this far-reaching scriptural principle, I explored through this study the extent to which Christian leaders embrace stewardship theology, how they practice it, and some of the challenges they face in its implementation.

Do Christian Leaders Believe They Should Be Stewards?

Let's start by looking at leaders' *beliefs* about stewardship. Do they know the theology and embrace it? To measure this, I asked a reasonably straightforward question that I think captures the essence of the teaching.

I asked Christian leaders whether they consider the financial resources at their disposal at work to really be "God's resources."

Figure 2-1 summarizes their responses. In qualitative terms, the average response is about halfway between moderate and strong agreement. In quantitative terms, better than six in ten (60.5%) express the highest level of agreement with the Biblical tenet that financial resources are

Pay bills on time. Keep debt to a minimum. Trust the Lord to supply your needs. Pray about purchases. And give generously to the Lord's work.

Dr. Peter Nelson
CEO
Valley Veterinary Service
Pennsylvania

God's resources. Another three of ten also agree, but to a lesser extent. The sum total of disagreement of any kind

Figure 2-1
At work, I consider all the resources at my disposal to really be God's resources

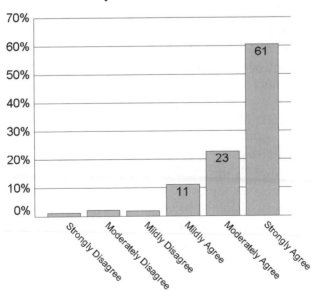

is a scant 5.5 percent. We can say, therefore, that the average Christian leader understands and believes the basic teaching that he or she is to be a steward in the workplace.

How Do Christian Leaders Practice Stewardship?

Next, there's the question of *applying* stewardship in the workplace. One might claim to believe stewardship theology, but does he or she operate any differently in the workplace from those who are less stewardship-oriented?

To estimate this, I asked four questions that implicate stewardship of money or time, comparing those who are more stewardship-oriented to those who are less stewardship-oriented.[2] I asked about paying bills: Is it a priority for the leader to pay all work-related bills on time? I asked about administration of his or her budget: Is the leader known to be a person who is "sensitive to budgetary constraints?" I asked about one's view of profits: Does the leader see profit as an end in itself or as a means to a greater end? I asked about stewardship of time and talent: Is it a priority for the leader to use his or her position to give something back to the local community?

As one might expect, there are differences between the high- and low-stewardship Christians in all of these areas. As shown in Figures 2-2 through 2-5, those who are more stewardship-oriented (i.e., those who say that "financial resources are God's resources") are significantly more likely to "strongly agree" with the four stewardship questions I asked. In particular, note the relatively large difference in the priority of timely bill paying (Figure 2-2). Although many in the low-

Figure 2-2
I make it a priority to pay all work-related bills on time

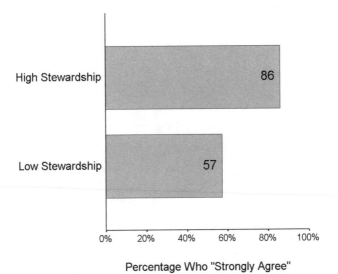

Percentage Who "Strongly Agree"

Figure 2-3
At work, people consider me to be a person who is sensitive to budgetary constraints

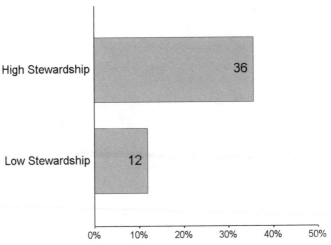

Percentage Who "Strongly Agree"

Figure 2-4
Profit is a means, not an end

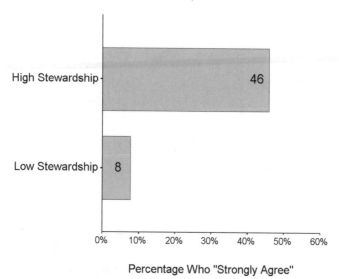

Percentage Who "Strongly Agree"

Figure 2-5
It is a priority for me to use my position to give
something back to the local community

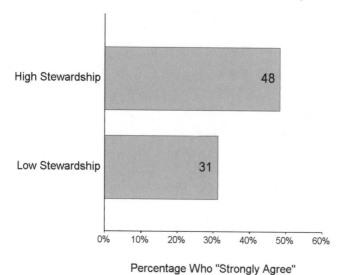

Percentage Who "Strongly Agree"

stewardship group avow they make this a priority (57%), almost all of those in the high-stewardship group (86%) strongly affirm this. Similarly, the high-stewardship group is about three times more likely to "strongly agree" that they are sensitive to budgetary constraints (Figure 2-3) and six times more likely to "strongly agree" with the scriptural tenet that "profit is a means, not an end" (Figure 2-4). Lastly, it seems that a stewardship mind-set may also spill over into the use of one's time and talent as well. Almost half of the stewards "strongly agree" that they use their position at work to give something back to the local community, whereas only about a third of their counterparts report this.

Clearly, more work needs to be done in this area to unpack both the belief structure and implementation of stewardship. However, this appears to be some important evidence that those who understand and embrace stewardship also "walk the talk," so to speak, administering their resources somewhat differently from those who are less inclined to see themselves as stewards.

There May Be a Greater Tension at the Top

For the final part of this analysis, I looked at leaders whose stewardship practices are most critical: those at the top of an organization. More specifically, I compared a sample of Christians in top management positions (vice-president level or higher—about 60% of our sample) to those holding lower-level positions. Top managers overwhelmingly affirm that financial

The higher up the corporate ladder people go, the less apparent their Christian walk seems to be. There's more pressure to conform.

Kenneth Lomax
President
Performance Improvement Network
California

resources are God's resources and they are *more likely* to enthusiastically affirm this than are the leaders in lower positions (88% to 77% in strong agreement). When it comes to the application of this belief, though, top managers are *no more likely* to make on-time bill paying a priority, *no more likely* to say they are known for being sensitive to budgetary constraints, *no more likely* to view profit as a means rather than an end, and *only marginally more likely* to say they use their position to give back to the local community.[3] This suggests (but certainly is not intended to prove) that although those higher up in the organization more strongly affirm their responsibility to be a steward, they may not *in practice* be better stewards. Stated differently, among top managers, there may be more of a gap between belief and application. Why might this be the case? I would suggest that *the challenge of being a steward may be more pronounced as one becomes more responsible for organizational performance.*

If this were the case, it would surely be ironic since it is at this job level where good stewardship arguably becomes most essential. Top managers in any organization are the individuals who have the greatest influence over budget allocation and organizational strategy. However, pressures from competitors, shareholders, creditors, boards of directors and other powerful entities may create significant, more tenacious obstacles to stewardship in high-level decision-making.

Still, *it is important not to lose sight of the fact that overall, committed Christians in top management are inclined to be stewards.* Christians at the top see more clearly than others that financial resources are God's resources. That's encouraging and it's a prerequisite for the implementation of this theology. But Christian leaders and aspiring Christian leaders should be vigilant. Whether

Do not try to undercut your suppliers' prices after you have given your word. Always pay for supplies by the agreed upon date. Do this even if you have to borrow money against your line of credit.

Fred Bolton
President
West Virginia Pipeline, Inc.

employed in business, in the public sector, or in traditional ministry, faithful stewardship may be increasingly difficult as one ascends the organizational ladder.

Serving the Better Master

In the world of business, the traditional presupposition is that money comes first. To generate and increase profit is the primary purpose of a for-profit business. At least, that's the conventional wisdom echoed by a preponderance of Wall Street.

A divergent perspective was advanced on the mount as Jesus taught: "No one can serve two masters. Either he will hate the one and love the other, or he will be devoted to the one and despise the other. You cannot serve both God and Money" (Matthew 6:24). Jesus offers a straightforward directive—choose your priority. There is no middle ground. Choosing either God or money precludes putting the other first.

Choosing God, in this context, means conceptualizing our financial resources, our talents, our time and our other blessings as God's property and God's providence. That's an essential first step toward genuine stewardship. It's a step that entails a confession that we own nothing, and as such, it requires humility. It's a step that entails enduring and answering the objections of some co-workers and friends, and as such, it requires courage. Ultimately, it's a step whose permanence entails continually seeing the world as God sees it, and as such, it requires grace and sanctification.

Herein lies the key to long-term stewardship. Successful stewardship is not achieved through a commitment to adopt a set of practices. It's achieved through the nurturing of one's relationship with God—a nurturing that has as one outgrowth, the grace to faithfully manage what rightfully belongs to Him. I suspect that many of the stewards in our sample learned this long ago.

Notes

1. The tenet that God owns everything and that we merely manage that which He has entrusted to us can be found, for example, in the following Scriptures: "The earth is the Lord's and everything in it, the world and all who live in it" (Psalm 24:1); "everything in heaven and earth is yours" (1 Chronicles 29:11); "for the world is mine, and all that is in it" (Psalm 50:12). Most prominently, perhaps, in the New Testament, Jesus makes this instruction plain in the parable of the talents (Matthew 25, Luke 19).

2. The measure of "high stewardship" for this analysis is moderate or strong agreement with the statement "At work, I consider the financial resources at my disposal to really be God's resources." I define "low stewardship" as disagreement at any level with this statement. I assumed that those who "mildly agree" with this statement could not be categorized as either "high" or "low" stewardship, so I excluded these individuals for the purpose of this analysis. I should also note that the low stewardship group constitutes only sixteen leaders, so I exercised caution when interpreting these data. However, I did find statistically significant differences even though one group is very small (i.e., despite the high probability of a Type II Error). This suggests that the differences I identified are indeed real.

3. In more technical terms, my hypothesis tests found a statistically significant difference at the five percent level for the belief question, but no significant differences in any of these other areas except for the "give back to the community" item, where a small difference between the two groups was statistically significant at the ten percent level.

CHAPTER 3

BUSINESS ACUMEN

CHRISTIAN LEADERS REPORT THEY'RE WISE AS SERPENTS (BUT COULD USE HELP BEING "HARMLESS AS DOVES")

How well equipped are Christian leaders to successfully manage and grow an organization? Are they good at what they do? Do they have a vision for where they want to take the organization, a plan to get there and some tools for tracking their progress? Can they solve problems and get results? As they pursue these things, to what extent do they exhibit Christlike character? This chapter presents some answers, identifying areas of strength and weakness in Christians' business acumen.

Customer Orientation

The extent to which one is "customer oriented" is an important thermometer of business acumen. It's a quality—actually, a disposition—that simply cannot be overstated. Whether the "customer" is an individual purchaser of goods and services, another organization, a student in one's school or a congregant in one's pew, identifying and meeting the needs of that customer is elemental to the survival and growth of the organization.

Christian leaders seem to know this maxim well. As shown in Chapter 1, Figure 1-2, customers are first among stakeholders. Almost two out of every three Christian leaders (63.1%) rank customer needs first, with another twenty-five percent giving customers the silver medal. Only three percent rank customers' needs any lower than third place.[1] Seemingly, customer priority is the standard for more than just the Christians who are peddling Pop-Tarts®. It's a disposition that transcends workplace contexts.

> If you're speaking to a customer, the customer is always right. If you have any doubt, the customer is always right.
>
> Laurel "Rocky" Peterson
> Owner
> Rancho Ybaura Christian Camp
> California

Vision, Planning and Goal Measurement

Let's next consider some basic managerial issues. This is not intended to be a comprehensive examination of all managerial skills and tools (the survey would have been far too long); rather, it explores a few larger issues from which we can draw inferences about professional acumen.

First, given the widely-recognized significance of having a "vision"—a purpose, a direction, a mental picture of what the future can and should look like—I asked these leaders whether they have a *clear long-term vision* for where they are taking the work group or organization. Second, I asked about a pillar of managerial success, the practice of *planning*. It's elemental to efficient and effective implementation, but not every leader makes the time for it. Do Christian leaders consider the critical managerial function of planning to be a high priority for them? Do they set goals and courses of action to pursue those goals? Third, I asked about their ability to *measure goal attainment*. Absent good measures, a leader cannot see clearly what's working and what's not. His or her ability to diagnose and solve problems is inhibited. Simply stated, measurement of progress and goal attainment is basic to continuous improvement.

> *If we truly want to be a Christian leader in our workplace, we need to look to God for a vision - a plan to take the employees, the product and the company to a new level.*
>
> John F. Price, Jr.
> Captain
> U.S. Air Force
> North Dakota

Overall, Christian leaders do report significant competence in these crucial areas of management. *In fact, in each area, a large majority of leaders "strongly" or "moderately" affirm that these are regular practices for them.* We get a further indication of their proficiency from the comparison in Table 3-1. Especially in the areas of planning and measuring goal attainment, Christian leaders are confident that they are implementing some of the basics of sound managerial practice.

Of course, we can also see from Table 3-1 that, as with any group of leaders, there is room for improvement. The vision, for some, could be clearer. The metrics for pursuing goals could be more available and more valid. Not all Christian leaders report expertise in these areas. A further analysis showed that this is particularly true for those with less managerial experience.

Table 3-1
Vision, Planning and Goal Measurement

	"Strongly Agree" Percent	Mild to Strong Disagree Percent
I have a clear long-term (three-ten year) vision for where I'd like to take my work group, department or organization	37%	13%
"Planning"-identifying and selecting goals and courses of action-is a high priority for me at work	52%	5%
I have good measures of how well my work group, department or organization is meeting its goals	31%	9%

It's also particularly true for those employed in *Christian non-profit organizations*, whether those organization are churches, schools, charities or other ministries. The leaders in those organizations are no less customer-oriented and no less confident about getting results or solving problems, but they do report less success with planning, goal measurement and especially long-term vision. Accordingly, the person laboring in full-time vocational Christian service might want to make some time to develop a clearer vision and to fine-tune his or her managerial skills. Many of these leaders are already overworked and may not feel they have the time for such things, but this is an investment of time that yields an abundant harvest in added efficiency and more effective service to God—rich dividends indeed.

Getting Results & Solving Problems

What are some work-related *outcomes* for Christian leaders? In particular, do the people around them at work think they can "solve problems" and "get results"? The answer to both questions for the vast majority is "yes"— an emphatic "yes!" in fact. Four out of ten leaders (41%) strongly agree with both questions.

Provide customers with a reliable and safe product; treat and compensate employees fairly, and produce an adequate return for those who have invested their hard-earned money in the business. In my opinion, it doesn't get any more Christian than that.

Joseph Schuh
Director of Planning
Orange and Rockland Utilities
New Jersey

Ninety-nine out of one hundred agree, at least to some extent, that they are known for getting results. And *every one of them* agrees at some level that they are known for solving problems. Although these are not actual measures of their competence (they are perceptions), it's evident that this group is reasonably confident in their abilities at work.

Wise as Serpents, but . . .

As revealed in Figure 3-1, there's other news to report that hangs in tension with these leaders' ability to get the job done. They responded to a series of questions regarding how others perceive them at work, including questions about their demeanor in dealing with people. It seems that although Christian leaders report they are essentially "as wise as serpents" (Matthew 10:16, NKJV) in the performance realm, they do not always get there by being "as harmless as doves." That is, they report significant challenges when asked whether others at work consider them to be a "patient" person or a "gentle"

Figure 3-1
"At work, people consider me to be a person who..."

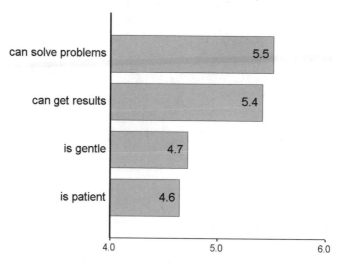

Mildly Agree (4.0), Moderately Agree (5.0), Strongly Agree (6.0)

person. Their averages in both of these areas fall below "moderate" agreement—a finding that stands in sharp contrast to their self-portrait on getting results and solving problems. Moreover, a noteworthy proportion (around 15%) *disagree* that others on the job see these virtues in them.

> *Take a deep breath and pray for guidance before saying anything critical or harsh.*
>
> Anonymous Respondent
> Attorney
> California

The story here is not that Christian leaders aren't patient or gentle people. They may be, on average, since a majority of these leaders say that, to some extent, they typically display both patience and gentleness at work. Rather, *the story is that Christian leaders report more success in personal performance areas than they do in critical areas of character.* They are, by their own admission, more adept at getting results and solving problems than they are exhibiting fundamental fruit of the Spirit virtues.

This may be an important reminder for Christians—a reminder that will likely ring true for many. As we pursue the very worthwhile ends of results, performance and problem solving, we need to do so in a way that faithfully represents the One who is exceedingly patient with us and who describes Himself as "gentle and humble in heart" (Matthew 11:29).

Notes

1. These results are no different when comparing leaders in the for-profit and not-for-profit sectors.

CHAPTER 4

UNCONVENTIONAL MANAGEMENT TOOLS

LEADERS WHO SEEK FIRST THE KINGDOM OF GOD HAVE MANY THINGS ADDED

Scripture offers a wealth of advice to the manager. Both the Old and New Testaments are replete with instruction about financial management, as well as human relations principles for managing employees, relating to customers and dealing properly with all those around us. Many Christian resources speak to these issues. One of the first and most widely read is Larry Burkett's *Business By the Book* (Thomas Nelson, 1990). Similarly, we find gospel lessons about the attitudes and behaviors of a master manager in another popular book, *The Management Methods of Jesus* (Thomas Nelson, 1996). From the Old Testament, the wisdom of the very practical "Book of Proverbs" has been tapped for managers in *Management by Proverbs: Applying Timeless Wisdom in the Workplace* (Moody Press, 1999).

Among most Christians, the notion that scripture can be applied to leadership, to management and to everything else we do in the workplace appears to be a non-controversial point. Also accepted, we'll see below, is the belief that taking scripture's advice is actually "useful" in management, although some Bible terrain is considered especially fertile for harvesting.

Besides scripture, a second unconventional "management tool" that we'll look at in this chapter is prayer. Notwithstanding the increasingly hostile climate for workplace prayer, Christians continue to pray as a means to better leadership and management. The striking news here is that there is a positive association between prayer and getting results as a leader. Consistent with a growing empirical literature on the effectiveness of prayer,[1] I found some superior workplace outcomes for those leaders who pray more often. The second half of the chapter will detail this finding.

Scripture as a Useful Management Tool

The Christian leaders I polled are, for the most part, a Biblically literate group. On average, they have "significant familiarity with the Bible and could explain its storyline and many of its doctrines and moral principles." So given that they know something about the Bible, to what extent do they agree that the Bible is a useful management tool? More narrowly, what about the usefulness of two areas of scripture often quoted in Christian business resources: the four Gospels (collectively) and the Book of Proverbs?

Not surprising, Christian leaders do affirm the utility of the Bible, the Gospels and Proverbs in the workplace. They are in "moderate" to "strong" agreement that each is a "useful management tool." Moreover, only about two

> *Study God's word every day, apply these principles of scripture to decision making and stay in prayer.*
>
> Charlotte Fish
> Director
> South Mountain Christian Camp
> North Carolina

percent express any level of disagreement (mild to strong) in each area.

There is some noteworthy diversity to report, though. First, there are significant differences in the enthusiasm Christians have for applying various scriptures at work. Figure 4-1 presents the percentage of leaders who "strongly agree" with each statement about scriptural usefulness. Almost four out of five (78%) strongly agree that the Bible is a useful tool in management. Fewer (71%) strongly agree that Proverbs is

Figure 4-1
Useful Management Tools

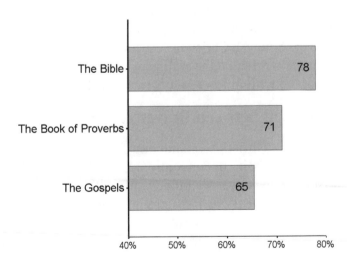

Percentage Who "Strongly Agree"

useful, and even fewer (65%) strongly agree that the Gospels are useful as a management tool.

This latter finding is especially salient. Why the gap between "Bible" usefulness and the "Gospels'" usefulness? Perhaps some consider non-gospel areas of scripture to be of greater value to the leader than are the Gospels. But beyond this relative comparison, why are fewer than two out of three enthusiastic about the Gospels' relevance for management? Aren't the words and the role modeling of Jesus *indispensable* lessons for us in the workplace? Christian leaders are somewhat divided on this question.

Looking a little closer at that division, longer-term Christians (twenty or more years in the faith) are more convinced about the Gospels' utility at work. More than seven out of ten (71%) long-term Christians strongly agree that the Gospels are useful management tools as compared to fewer than six out of ten (57%) for those younger in the faith. It may then be the case that as Christians mature, they increasingly see the applicability of gospel lessons in leadership and perhaps, in life more generally. Younger Christian leaders may therefore want to read the writing on the wall here—or perhaps just read more of the writing from Matthew, Mark, Luke and John.

Connection between Prayer & Performance

From a Christian standpoint, prayer is another important, albeit unconventional, tool for leaders. Christian leaders overwhelmingly affirm this, with almost four out of five (79%) in strong agreement with the statement, "Prayer is a useful management tool." Beyond that, another 14% "moderately agree" with the statement.

Can prayer affect our performance? Does God intervene in response to prayer to make us better, more effective leaders? The question is beyond dispute scripturally.

Pray on the way to the office. Pray about any major decision. And thank God at the end of the day for His help.

Reverend N.I. Bunn
Senior Pastor
Living Bread Ministries Church
Illinois

God promises us empowerment and blessing if we, with right motive, ask for them (see, for example, Matthew 7:8–11, Matthew 6:33).

Consistent with these scriptural promises, this research finds four connections between prayer and performance. As compared to other Christian leaders surveyed, *those who believe prayer to be a useful management tool and who say they seek God's will through prayer*:

1. Report a clearer *long-term vision* at work
2. Report being more *efficient* at work
3. Report more often that they are known for being able to *solve problems* at work
4. Report more often that they are known for *getting results* at work[2]

I think the most important reason that I am better today than in the past is because I try to pray on all my decisions.

Ed Jones
President
Dohrman Printing Co.
New Jersey

Vision. Efficiency. Problem solving. Results. These are significant outcomes for any leader. It's a list that reads like the ideal resume. Furthermore, there is another outcome experienced by the more prayer-centered leaders—an arguably more important outcome, from a divine perspective. They report greater success in displaying *Christian character* (the fruit of the Spirit) in the workplace. In particular, they especially report greater joy, inner peace, kindness, generosity, patience, faithfulness and love. It seems that the ideal resume just got that much better.[3]

I pray everyday that the Lord will help me treat all of my patients with compassion and love.

David Yamaguchi, DDS
California

These are important results. Reliance upon prayer appears to be related to both business acumen and more consistent virtue: *competence and character.* These are precisely the two dimensions that should distinguish believers in the workplace. As I'll discuss in more detail in chapter 8, prayer may in fact be a critical pathway to genuine success in leadership.

Notes

1. For a synopsis of this literature, see Matthews, D. A. (1998), *The Faith Factor.* New York: Viking, or Poloma. M. M. and Pendleton, B. F. (1991). "The Effects of Prayer and Prayer Experiences on Measures of General Well Being," *Journal of Psychology and Theology,* 1, 71–83.
2. All results from correlation analysis and significant at the 5% level or better.
3. All correlations are significant at the 5% level. The magnitude of the correlations between prayer-centeredness and Christian character qualities ranges from 0.119 (patient person at work) to 0.328 (loving person at work).

CHAPTER 5

WORKPLACE WITNESSES

SOME CHRISTIAN LEADERS MAKE DISCIPLES AT ALL WORK STATIONS

The New Testament teaches that Christians are to share the Good News of the Gospel and to "make disciples of all nations" (Matthew 28:19). There is no Biblical exemption for the workplace or any other venue. However, the appropriateness and the priority of verbal witnessing in the workplace is the area where we see the most variation in attitude among Christian leaders.

How much of a priority is verbal witnessing for Christian leaders? It's a significant one, for some, as indicated in Figure 5-1. About one in four "strongly agree" that witnessing is a priority for them at work. Another two in four also agree—but with less enthusiasm—that it's a priority. Overall, Christian leaders appear to embrace the idea of everyday evangelism, viewing witnessing as something they should do on a regular basis.

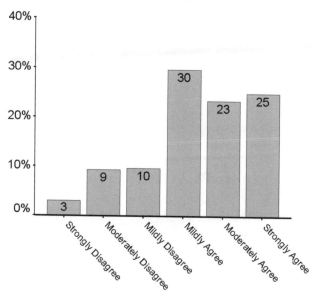

Figure 5-1
"Verbally Sharing Christ Is a Priority
for Me at Work"

That's not to say that they embrace evangelism everyday, though. Of those who say that they do witness at work, the frequency of that witnessing varies tremendously, from daily to less than once a month, as noted in Figure 5-2. Approximately one in seven leaders witness on a daily basis—about the same ratio as those who witness once a week, once a month and less than once a month. We'll see next what explains some of this variance.

> I come into contact with many more spiritually needy people than my pastor does. God has given me this business as a platform for ministry.
>
> Robert Norland
> President
> Association Reserves, Inc.
> California

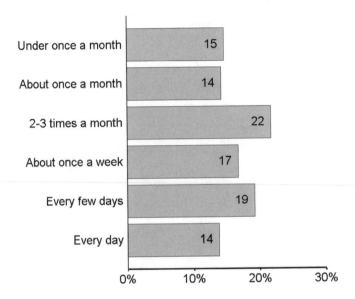

Figure 5-2
"How Often Do You Verbally Witness at Work?"
(percentage of those who do witness at work)

What's the Profile of the Workplace Witness?

Male versus Female

Interestingly, women in this study are less likely to say that workplace witnessing is a priority. In fact, they are more than twice as likely to *disagree* with the statement, "Verbally sharing Christ is a priority for me at work."

Top Management versus Lower Management

It is also the case that those in a top management position are, on average, more likely to say that witnessing is a priority and to witness more frequently. It may be, then, that as one feels less threatened from above in the organization, one feels freer to share the gospel.[1]

Stated differently, many Christians in middle or lower management may feel more pressured to keep their beliefs to themselves. In fact, almost none of our middle or lower managers (4% as compared to 17% in top management) say that they witness everyday.

For-Profit versus Not-for-Profit

There are negligible witnessing differences in for-profit versus non-profit organizations, although as one would expect, leaders in churches and para-church ministries do witness more frequently. Overall, though, it doesn't seem that employment in the for-profit sector has squelched these leaders' passion for evangelism.

> *Our lives may, in some cases, be the only Bible that our customers read.*
>
> Ken Verheyer
> President
> Precision Chemical Cleaning Services
> California

Christian Maturity Is the Key

One might expect to find a relationship between the number of years a person has been a Christian and that person's evangelism priority and frequency, but there is no evidence of this relationship. That is, there is no evidence that more years as a Christian leads to more witnessing in the workplace and no evidence that longer-term Christians assume roles as ambassadors of the faith.

However, that's not the same as saying that Christian *maturity* is unconnected to witnessing. It's inextricably connected. The profile of the workplace witness—independent of gender, job level, for-profit organization or veteran Christian status—is one of a *God-centered individual*. This is a prayerful person who enjoys an active and growing relationship with God, who has a relatively conservative view of scripture and who usually has a lot of Bible knowledge. Workplace witnessing, it would seem, is not something that just any Christian will do because it's commanded in a

I try to live as enthusiastically and reverently as possible. No one gets to walk by me without being given a smile and a hello.

Hugh Root
Director of Continuing Education
Mass Mutual
Florida

Matthean passage. Rather, witnessing from nine to five is a natural outgrowth of a stronger relationship with God.

Witnessing is only one of many outgrowths, though. This same God-centered individual, when compared with other Christians surveyed, tends to experience more success with fruit of the Spirit virtues at work, tends to be a better steward of financial resources and tends to be more employee-oriented. As we'll see in the next chapter, there is a distinct leadership and management style of the "fruit of the Spirit" leader, one dimension of which is a willingness to share verbally the pearl of Good News that he or she has found.

Notes

1. This finding may stand in contrast with our finding in chapter 2 that top managers may be more tempted to reject stewardship because of organizational pressures. Perhaps top managers feel freer to speak their beliefs, but feel less free to act on them at the expense of organizational resources.

CHAPTER 6

"FRUIT OF THE SPIRIT" LEADERS

PRIORITIES & PRACTICES OF MODEL CHRISTIAN LEADERS

Pursuing "Fruit of the Spirit" Leadership

Why pursue "fruit of the Spirit" leadership? The answer is not necessarily obvious. Therefore, before we dive into the findings about this leadership style, we should begin with its theological underpinnings.

The starting point is the elemental teaching that Christians are called to integrate their faith into daily living. The Christian life is not a dualistic one that relegates one's spiritual life to the pews while living independent of God elsewhere. Faith and life are to be seamless.

Christian scripture speaks generously to this issue, both in the Old and New Testament, encouraging the believer to "commit to the Lord whatever you do" (Proverbs 16:3), to "do it all for the glory of God"

(1 Corinthians 10:31) and to let your "light shine before men, that they may see your good deeds and praise your Father in heaven" (Matthew 5:16; also Colossians 3:23–24, 1 John 2:6, Psalm 37:5). In Galatians 5, the Apostle Paul goes farther, providing Christians with *nine distinct measures* of the extent to which God is operating within them daily. Widely cited and collectively called the "fruit of the Spirit," the nine measures are as follows: "love, joy, peace, patience, kindness, goodness, faithfulness, gentleness and self-control" (Galatians 5:22–23).

These dispositions and behaviors are indicators of Christian maturity, *a reflection of God working in and through the believer.* Christians claim this, in part, because Jesus Himself taught: "No branch can bear fruit by itself; it must remain in the vine. Neither can you bear fruit unless you remain in me" (John 15:4). Accordingly, if one seeks to know what Christian character looks like in daily life—including one's life as a leader—Paul's "fruit of the Spirit" list may be among the most succinct portrayals.

These scriptural teachings on the faith-life nexus raise a host of questions for the Christian leader. It is one thing to say that Christians should strive to be fruit of the Spirit leaders, but it is quite another to know

> *I will not be satisfied with simply clicking off tasks or meeting objectives. I want to live a useful life.*
>
> Scott Mabry
> VP Operations and Technology
> First Data Corp.
> Georgia

what that actually means on a day-to-day basis. Even more basic than that, it is one thing to say that Christians are to grow in the fruit of the Spirit, but it is quite another to actually make progress—or even know where to begin, for that matter.

On the former question (day-to-day implementation), there is no research to date. This chapter presents the inaugural investigation in that realm by first looking at where Christian leaders say they are stronger and weaker on the fruit, and by then examining the specific priorities and practices inherent in those who are fruit of the Spirit leaders. Some of those priorities and practices are obvious. Others might be a little surprising.

On the latter question—the question about how to grow—there is a lot more information publicly available. From academic texts to popular Christian magazines, there is significant commentary about how to cultivate fruit. Chapters 7 and 8 add to that commentary, presenting this study's conclusions about growth.

Where Do Leaders Say They Are Stronger & Weaker?

Using nine different survey items, corresponding to the nine fruit of the Spirit, I inquired into each leader's perception of how he or she is viewed by his or her co-workers. In particular, I asked them whether the people at work consider them to be a "loving" person, a "joyful" person, etc., all the way down to a person who is "self-controlled."

Overall, Christian leaders claim that they are doing reasonably well in most of these areas. For each one of the nine fruit, the average response was at the very least to "mildly agree" that they display the virtue in question. There are some intriguing differences, though, as shown in Figure 6-1.

Figure 6-1
Where Christians Are Stronger and Weaker on the Fruit of the Spirit in the Workplace

At Work, People Consider Me to Be ...

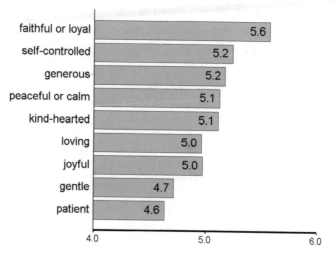

Mildly Agree (4.0), Moderately Agree (5.0), Strongly Agree (6.0)

The bar chart depicts the Christian leader as one who believes he or she is strong on "faithfulness," struggling a bit with "patience" and "gentleness" and moderately exhibiting the other fruit.[1] Indeed, it would appear that Christian leaders experience a genuine imbalance across these nine virtues—what John Stott has labeled "lop-sided" Christianity.[2]

> On Sunday, our Bible lesson teaches that all have sinned. Yet on Monday, we expect our employees to be perfect.
>
> Terry Tonkin
> Program Director
> Magellan Health
> Virginia

How Does the Fruit of the Spirit Leader Lead?

Table 6-1 summarizes the leadership style of the fruit of the Spirit leader. Those who score highest[3] on the "fruit of the Spirit" are more accessible than others, reporting more often that: "My employees would say that they can talk to me about anything." They are also more likely to say that they try to "criticize with care" and that it's their job to quickly resolve conflict among their employees.

Table 6-1
A Summary of the Management Style
of the "Fruit of the Spirit" Leader

Employee Management Issues

- Very accessible and approachable
- Try to resolve conflict among their subordinates quickly
- Are careful to "criticize with care"
- Make it a practice to praise/ encourage employees
- Reward both performance and effort when giving a raise

Customer Orientation

- Customer is by far the number one stakeholder
- Avoid overselling what their product or service can do

Financial Stewardship

- Consider all financial resources to be God's resources
- View profit as a means rather than as an end
- Significant sensitivity to budgetary constraints
- Make it a priority to use their position to give back to the local community
- Pay all work-related bills on time and have a general sensitivity to suppliers' needs

Other Business Acumen Issues

- Good long term (3–10 year) vision
- Good measures of goal attainment
- Consider themselves to be problem solvers

55

The fruit of the Spirit leaders further report that they make a practice of rewarding employees with encouragement and praise and, when it comes to giving a raise, they are more likely than others to increase pay based on a worker's effort. Performance certainly matters to them, but they value and repay hard work on the part of their subordinates.

People are always more important than the task.
Dottie Wobb
Executive Director
Hope Pregnancy Centers
Florida

Fruit of the Spirit leaders also consider themselves to be stewards, not owners, of organizational resources. Rooted in the theology that all financial resources are God's resources, these leaders view profit as a means rather than as an end, they report greater budget sensitivity than do other leaders in the sample and they report that they make it a higher priority to use their position to give back to the local community.

In the same vein, this notion of stewardship appears to spill over into dealings with suppliers. Fruit of the Spirit leaders say, more than do others in our sample, that they make it a priority to pay all of their work-related bills on time. Moreover, when ranking the needs of stakeholders, these leaders tend to be more sensitive to their suppliers' needs as compared to other Christian leaders we surveyed.

Eat oatmeal and beans, but pay your bills.
Steven Emmerson
V.P. Marketing
Poly Cello
New Brunswick, Canada

Stakeholder one, however, is the customer. *Even more so* than their counterparts in this study, fruit of the Spirit leaders report that the needs of customers come first among stakeholders. Relatedly, they are in greater agreement with the statement: "I avoid overselling what my product or service can do." Indeed, the fruit of the Spirit leader is highly customer-focused.

Lastly, there are three other business acumen variables that distinguish the fruit of the Spirit leaders from other Christian leaders. The former report greater long-term (three to ten year) vision than do their counterparts and they say more often that they have "good measures of goal attainment." Additionally, fruit of the Spirit leaders consider themselves better problem solvers than do others.

What to Expect in a Secular Work Environment

It may be argued that, in some ways, the profile of the fruit of the Spirit leader does not align well with contemporary thinking about good leadership and management. There will likely be tension in this person's work life since some of his or her values and priorities may not overlap with the values and priorities of the organization. Thinking about money as God's resource rather than the stockholder's or business owner's resource is one example. Making it a priority to use one's position to give back to the local community is another. In the realm of employee management, the fruit of the Spirit leader rewards effort, but there is to date no empirically established connection between employee performance and paying people based on effort. In fact, some have claimed that this is a counter-productive practice.[4] As far

> *My daily walk is observed continually by my co-workers and it must demonstrate the fruit of the Spirit. If it doesn't, my talk means nothing.*
>
> Dale Wicker
> Quality Manager
> Hella Electronics
> Michigan

as paying bills on time, this is generally good business practice, but it may also be argued that under some circumstances, it is more prudent from a cash flow standpoint to pay suppliers on the same timetable that customers pay the company (regardless of whether this is "on time" for the account payable).

In other ways, the above profile is *highly consistent* with contemporary thinking about good leadership and management practice. Best-selling business books repeatedly encourage a strong customer-orientation,[5] the elimination of barriers between management and labor,[6] the careful and expedient resolution of conflict[7] and richly rewarding employees with praise.[8] Similarly, having a clear long-term vision, good measures of goal attainment, budget sensitivity and strong problem solving skills are fundamentals for the efficiency and success of the work group that one leads. Indeed, these outcomes, all of which are associated with Christian character in this study, should contribute to maximizing work group and organizational performance.

Consequently, this portrait of the mature Christian leader—one who exhibits the fruit of the Spirit in the workplace—is, from an organizational perspective, two-dimensional. On one hand, it is a portrait of a person whose decisions may sometimes conflict with those in the organization who do not share the same worldview. On the other hand, it is a portrait of a competent, customer-oriented, employee-oriented, community-oriented individual who has the potential to be a significant asset to the organization. Overall, it would seem that the pros clearly outweigh the cons since, from a Christian standpoint, the most important stakeholder—God Himself—desires the cultivation and application of these virtues.

So, then, one question lingers: how do we get there? We turn now in the last two chapters to the obstacles and pathways to becoming a more godly, more "fruitful" leader.

***

Notes

1. One should be cautious about generalizing too far with this ranking, however, since this is a public context. For instance, whereas Christians may display a decent level of "self-control" in the workplace, their disposition may be different in a private setting like the home. Consequently, Figure 6-1 should be viewed as public fruit bearing.

2. John R.W. Stott, *Baptism and Fullness: The Work of the Holy Spirit Today*, (Downers Grove, Ill.: InterVarsity Press, 1976), 77.

3. By "score highest" on the fruit of the Spirit, we're simply using the individual's average response for the nine fruit of the Spirit items.

4. See, for example, the following classic article: Kerr, S.: 1975, 'On the Folly of Rewarding A, While Hoping for B,' *Academy of Management Journal*, 18, 769–783.

5. Blanchard, Kenneth: 1993, *Raving Fans: A Revolutionary Approach to Customer Service*, (William Morrow and Co., New York, NY); Whiteley, Richard C.: 1993, *The Customer Driven Company: Moving from Talk to Action*, (Perseus Press, Cambridge MA).

6. Case, John F: 1996, *Open Book Management: The Coming Business Revolution* (Harperbusiness, San Francisco CA); Stack, Jack 1994, *The Great Game of Business*, (Currency/Doubleday, New York, NY).

7. Fisher, Roger, Willian Ury and Bruce Patton: 1981, *Getting to Yes: Negotiating and Agreement Without Giving In*, (Penguin, New York, NY).

8. Nelson, Bob: 1994, *1001 Ways to Reward Employees*, Workman Publishing, (New York NY); Buckingham, Marcus and Curt Coffman: 1999, *First Break all the Rules: What the World's Greatest Managers Do Differently*, (Simon and Schuster, New York, NY).

CHAPTER 7

PRIMARY OBSTACLES TO CHRISTIAN LEADERSHIP

"Knowing" and "doing" are surely distinct entities. Legions of Christians traveling the circuitous road toward sanctification understand this well. We Christians may know what God wills us to do, but often we still don't do it.

Counted among those struggling with this "implementation gap" are some of the giants of the Bible. Philip Yancey notes this in his trenchant work, *I Was Just Wondering*, posing the question: "Why did King Solomon show such wisdom in writing the Proverbs and then spend the latter part of his life breaking those Proverbs?" We could add similar questions from Biblical history. Why did King David, a man who knew God's law as well as anyone of his day, sleep with Bathsheba anyway? Why did Peter, having recently confessed Jesus as the Christ, turn around and deny that he even knew Jesus? Why did Paul, after planting churches and preaching the Good News for years, say late in his ministry that he still couldn't stop himself from doing what is wrong (Romans 7)?

The answer is this: because these people, like all of us, stand in the dubious human tradition of being unwilling to always submit to God's will. Something's in the way—many things, actually. Some of these obstacles are internal to us; others are external. But every one of these obstacles separates knowing from doing. Every one prevents us from traveling God's higher road.

These obstacles, as we'll see in this chapter, are no less a problem for Christians in the contemporary workplace. We'll first look at some quantitative evidence of the implementation gap for Christian leaders and then turn to understanding that gap qualitatively, examining in more detail leaders' biggest obstacles to living the faith at work. Hopefully, seeing the obstacles of others more clearly will put us in a better position to identify and address our own obstacles, thus enabling us to more consistently do that which we know.

A Gap between What Christians Believe and What Christians Do at Work

Consider this: If someone has made a sincere personal commitment to Jesus Christ, would he or she also consider God to be the Boss at work? One might think so, but that's not always the case. What if we look exclusively at those who *do* strongly agree that God is their Boss at work? Would not that affirmation dominate their approach to selling, to employee management and to financial management? It should, but again, that's not always the case.

This isn't just conjecture. Figure 7-1 presents evidence to answer these questions. Looking across six

Figure 7-1
A Gap Between Knowing and Doing

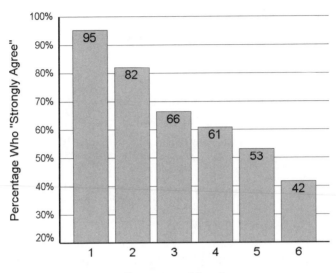

Statement Number

1. I have made a personal commitment to Jesus Christ that is still important in my life today
2. At work, God is my ultimate Boss
3. I avoid overselling what my product or service can do
4. At work, I consider the financial resources at my disposal to really be God's resources
5. It is a high priority for me to serve my employees
6. Profit is a means, not an end

different statements, although almost all (95%) Christian leaders strongly agree that they have made a personal commitment to Christ, fewer (82%) strongly agree that God is their ultimate boss at work. Furthermore, when it comes to what are arguably Christ-centered approaches to sales (Statement 3: avoiding overselling), employee management (Statement 5: serving employees) and financial management (Statement 4 and 6: financial resources are God's and profit is a means), the percentages become smaller still. The gap between knowing and doing, as shown in Figure 7-1, in conjunction with many similar findings from chapters 1 through 6, illustrate the continuing challenge for Christians to walk the talk in the workplace.

In light of this gap, the next logical question is: "Why do Christian leaders stumble?" What trips them up? What should they guard against when trying to be God-honoring leaders? *What are the primary obstacles to applying the Christian faith at work?* I conducted interviews with 152 leaders to find out.[1]

The Primary Obstacles

The leaders I consulted about these obstacles come from various backgrounds and have a wide range of management experience. The interviewed group is also reasonably balanced by gender, with 40 percent of the responses coming from female leaders.

Specifically, I asked the straightforward, open-ended question: "For you personally, what are the greatest obstacles to consistently living your faith at work?" Their responses were introspective. They were humble. They seemed candid. Collectively, the responses confirmed both a diversity of problems as well as some significant commonalities. In sum, these leaders listed seventy-two distinct obstacles, all of which are enumerated in the appendix to this chapter. More helpful for our purposes here: as a group they pointed to a handful of the most pervasive and tenacious obstacles. As shown in Table 7-1, there appear to be more than rocks in the road to Christlike leadership. There are some genuine boulders as well. Let's take a look at them.

Table 7-1
For you personally, what are the greatest obstacles
to consistently living your faith at work?
Based on Responses from 152 Christian Leaders

Obstacle	Percentage of Leaders Reporting this Obstacle		
	All	Male	Female
Pride Issues (Total)	74.3	65.2	88.3
Reputation or "People-Pleasing"	17.1	9.8	28.3
Ambition/Career Striving for "Success"	9.2	10.9	6.7
Communication Issues (Total)	38.8	42.4	33.3
Can't Control My Tongue	15.8	18.5	11.7
Poor Conflict Resolution Skills	10.5	8.7	13.3
Not a Good Listener	6.6	8.7	3.3
Other Issues			
Miscellaneous Obstacles	24.3	22.8	26.7
Impatience	19.7	14.1	28.3
Task-orientation	14.5	16.3	11.7
Lack of Care for Others	13.1	13.0	13.3
Busyness	11.8	8.7	16.7
Not Good at Forgiveness	9.2	8.7	10.0
Corporate Culture	8.6	12.0	3.3
Don't Trust Others to Do the Job Right	5.9	3.3	10.0
Burnout	5.3	3.3	8.3
Ingratitude for What I Have	5.3	5.4	5.0

Pride

Foremost among these obstacles is "pride" in its myriad forms. It's the antithesis of God-centered humility, a humility personified by Jesus Christ. While a few leaders identified "pride" generally as an obstacle, most elaborated further, citing self-centeredness, an unwillingness to take advice, a mindset that they are "above" others, demands to be in control, refusing to trust God or to submit to Him, an unwillingness to accept criticism, a propensity to impose views on others and a refusal to trust others enough to delegate work. Both men and women put pride atop their obstacles list.

Reputation and Ambition

One could also include in the pride category obstacles like "concern for one's reputation" and "drive for success," but these are separated out in Table 7-1 given the significant frequency with which they appear. The reputation issue is a biggie, it seems. Call it concern for one's image. Call it a focus on "people-pleasing" over God-pleasing. Regardless the label, many Christians don't want to risk friendships and promotion opportunities for the sake of their faith. They also wrestle with ambition—the desire to climb higher and faster in their career—at the expense of a consistently Christlike disposition. Clearly, the potential social consequences and job consequences of taking one's faith seriously sometimes crowd God out of Christians' work lives.

> *Too often we are like Jonah, trying to choose our battles and minimize our risks.*
>
> John F. Price, Jr.
> Captain
> US Air Force
> North Dakota

Corporate Culture

Whereas ambition and concern for reputation are internal obstacles, the corporate culture—the environment in which one works—is an external obstacle with similar effects on one's character. Without vigilance, people can drift to become like those around them at work and some of our leaders recognize this problem. Adopting the assumptions of the secular organizations (e.g., assumptions about the way work should be done, the way to relate to people and how to make decisions) sometimes undermines one's ability to act like Jesus on the job and to make the decisions that He would make.

Communication Problems

Communication problems in their various forms, are also a major inhibitor. Cited in this general category are things like an unwillingness to communicate, an inability to criticize and poor listening skills. Relatedly, there is the issue of controlling one's tongue. Many report

I seem to often wake up agnostic and need to enter into a devotional time to reconnect with the Lord. If I forget...then I can get angry or abrupt and fail to treat vendors and suppliers with respect.

Stephen Garrison
Owner
Garrison Developments
California

difficulty here, saying that they are not gentle, they are not meek, they lose their temper too often, they are hypercritical or that they have a tendency to gossip. This affirms and supplements the finding in chapter 3 that Christians could benefit from some improvement in the area of gentleness. Chapter 3 also reported that patience might be a problem for Christian leaders and indeed, a substantial proportion of both men and women cite impatience as an obstacle in communication.

Conflict Resolution Skills

Also related to communication issues, both genders cite poor conflict resolution skills as a barrier to living their faith at work. These Christians understand that they are called to be "peacemakers" (Matthew 5:9), but many avoid or ignore conflict, saying they "don't like to deal with it" or that they are "not very good at resolving interpersonal problems."

Busyness or Overcommitment

Busyness or overcommitment showed up frequently in the survey as well. It's a problem that transcends genders, but in this sample, more women than men indicated that their frenetic darting from task to task undermines their ability to care about and meet others' needs. Relatedly, leaders also report that the natural end of this busyness—burnout—also limits their witness.

Task or Financial Orientation

As shown in chapter 1, a challenge for the Christian manager is to balance concern for results with a concern for people. Many Christian leaders are apparently keenly aware that the former inhibits the latter for them.

Lack of Care for Others

This may be the other side of the task orientation coin. Clearly it would be impossible to love and serve others, and to put others' needs first, if one doesn't really care about those

I'd be a great manager if it weren't for the people.

Name Withheld
Chief Financial Officer
Georgia

other people. A notable proportion of those sampled stated outright that they have little compassion or care for those around them at work, precluding them from being authentic witnesses to the truth of God's love.

Beating the Obstacle Course

This is quite an array of obstacles, but for the Christian who is willing to work at it, this is one obstacle course that can be conquered.

Some of the impediments have reasonably obvious solutions. Busyness is remedied by adopting a simpler lifestyle—by choosing to do fewer things, by saying no to the lesser things in favor of excellence in doing the greater things. It's a choice, by God's grace, and myriad magazine articles and best-selling Christian books show that the power to beat busyness resides with you. Similarly, having poor conflict resolution skills can be addressed somewhat efficiently by learning about how to do this better and by practicing the techniques. Influential secular resources like *Getting to Yes* and *Getting Past No*,[2] as well as Christian resources like *The Peacemaker*[3] will take you to the next level in this area if you make the time to adopt and implement their recommendations. These are skills, and like any other skills, the more you practice them the more capable you become in conflict resolution.

But what about the other obstacles obstructing your path? What about pride, people pleasing, impatience, low compassion or a loose tongue? What about the tendency to be molded in the worldly image of a corporate culture? How does one remedy such obstinate problems? How does one finally move the boulders that have for decades blocked the road between knowing and doing? The next chapter presents what I hope will be some helpful answers.

Notes

1. Of these 152 leaders, 124 were new to this study, not part of the original sample of 328 leaders.
2. Fisher, Roger, William Ury and Bruce Patton: 1981, *Getting to Yes: Negotiating and Agreement Without Giving In*, (Penguin, New York, NY). Ury, William: 1991, *Getting Past No: Negotiating Your Way From Confrontation To Cooperation*, (Bantam Books, New York, NY).
3. Sande, Ken: 1997, *The Peacemaker: A Biblical Guide to Resolving Personal Conflict*, (Baker Books: Grand Rapids, MI).

Appendix to Chapter 7
Obstacles to Living the Faith at Work

Pride Issues

Self-centeredness
A "me-first" attitude
Won't listen to others/won't take advice from others
I don't take criticism well
Impose my views on others
I must be in control of the situation
Think in terms of a hierarchy of persons
Too much focus on my rights
Self-reliance
I lack trust in God/submission to God
Ignoring God
Making time for God
Not God-centered enough
I must be right all the time
Concern for my reputation
Fear of persecution
Desire to belong with the group
Ambition/drive for success/career orientation
Money and power/greed
Temporal focus

Communication Issues

Unwillingness to communicate
I'm unapproachable
Inability to criticize
Poor listening skills
Poor conflict resolution skills/don't like to deal with conflict
Can't control my tongue
Not gentle/not meek
Lack of self-control
Lose my temper often
Hyper-critical and judgmental
I gossip too much
I complain a lot
I speak too quickly
Not persuasive enough

Corporate Culture Issues

My corporate culture
Corporate policies
Organizational priorities
Hating my organization

Appendix to Chapter 7 (Continued)
Obstacles to Living the Faith at Work

Care for Others Issues

Don't care about others/no love for them

Don't want to serve people

Not employee oriented

Lack compassion

Not merciful

Task-Orientation Issues

Too focused on the task

Need to get work done/ produce

Rules oriented

Financially oriented

Busyness Issues

Too busy

Improper balance

Deadlines

Over commitment

Miscellaneous Issues

Unwillingness to forgive

I seek revenge

Impatience

Lack business skills/ experience/knowledge

Lack knowledge of what a Christian should do

Burnout

Ingratitude

Worry/anxiety

Don't get along with people

Subconscious discrimination on my part

Poor time management

Perfectionism

Laziness/procrastination

Budget is too small

I'm not generous

I don't trust employees to do it right

My secular professional training

Lack of a personal mission/ purpose

Lack of self-esteem/ confidence

No inner peace about life

No happiness or joy in my life

CHAPTER 8

THE SECRET TO BETTER
CHRISTIAN LEADERSHIP

So far in this book I've explored the priorities and practices of Christian leaders, I've profiled the model "fruit of the Spirit" leader, and I've identified the major stumbling blocks to becoming such a leader. What remains, though, is crucial: how to get from A to B, from where you are now to where God wants you to be. Seeing the obstacles clearly is an important part of the journey, but it's not enough. Seeing doesn't guarantee circumventing. It doesn't guarantee personal progress, spiritual growth, or "leadership success" in God's eyes.

But what does?

First, I should say that there's no quick-and-easy fix here. There's no magic wand that you can wave to assure sanctified leadership by next Monday morning. Contrary to what you might infer from reading certain magazine articles, hearing well-intended sermons, or picking up a popular book on the subject, no one can take three easy steps to become a God-honoring Christian leader. That's far too simplistic. Overcoming one's character flaws and one's very nature, not to mention a lifetime of bad habits, is one of the most challenging conundrums with which man has ever wrestled.

Today, though, we are the beneficiaries of all of that wrestling. Centuries of exegesis and examen have furnished us with perspective, with hope, with a way to remove the boulders in the road that takes us from knowing the faith to consistently and joyfully living the faith.

The first part of the solution is this: recognize that you're not strong enough to remove the boulders. On our own, we don't have the power to permanently beat things like pride, greed, ambition, impatience, concern for reputation or lack of compassion. That, I think, is by God's design. God does not want us to pursue sanctification and Christian living by ourselves. Quite the opposite, God wants us to *depend on Him* to move the boulders for us.

That's a very different approach from the one tried by legions of Christians. Many have attempted to become Christian leaders—and have achieved quite patchy results—by learning about how Christianity applies to leadership or to various organizational functions like employee management, marketing or financial management. The problem with that is not necessarily with the books, classes and seminars themselves, but with the *exclusive reliance* on such resources. This myopic reliance ignores the foundational inward journey that must take place if one wants to consistently practice the things that one learns about in these books and in these educational venues.

Reading is not enough. Hearing is not enough. Knowing is not enough. Trying hard is not enough.

74

Making heart-felt vows to do better next time is not enough. What's required is something more, something deeper, something *relational*.

I'm not a fan of silver bullets, especially in the theological realm. But this much is true. If there's one "secret to success" in Christian leadership, it is that *we lead best when God is leading us*. That's far from a quick fix; rather, it's a declaration that God-honoring leadership doesn't happen because we try to make it happen. Successful leadership is a product of much groundwork, of much time spent with the One whom we are ultimately seeking to please. Making the right decisions at work, choosing the correct priorities, relating to people as Jesus would relate to them, performing with excellence no matter the task or the pay—all of the attitudes and behaviors to which Christians should aspire to in the workplace—happen more consistently when they are the outgrowth of an active and growing relationship with God.

When you make your relationship with God a priority in your life, correct attitudes and behaviors are an *automatic response* at work and everywhere else. They're instinctive and inevitable. The obstacles are still in proximity, but they are less of a nuisance because God confers on those close to Him a clearer vision to see the world as He sees it. You're more likely to live in continued cognizance of God's will, a cognizance that bulldozes your

> *One can be a successful business person and also be a faithful follower of Christ. But that will only happen if we decide to make Christ Number One and then make business align. It will not work the other way.*
>
> Steve Wilson
> President
> Storage Investors Management
> Florida

75

personal obstacles by keeping you mindful of what really matters in life. It's not a magic wand, but it is quite miraculous. You become a fundamentally different person, empowered to do things that you were never able to do in your own strength.

By contrast, when we do not give relationship with God top priority, the yoke of Christian leadership often seems arduous. It becomes a burden rather than a blessing because it contravenes what is intrinsic both to us and, often, to our work environments. As a result, considerable obstacles appear at every turn. We are tempted to live and work for ourselves and by our own rules. Career or paycheck may become an idol, leading to a busyness that only accelerates the downward spiral. Our values and priorities are more easily tossed about by the powerful waves of corporate culture. Desire to preserve friendships and to "fit in" become more important than friendship with God. The norms of the workplace govern the use of our tongue. An innate self-centeredness may desensitize us to the needs of others. Under these circumstances, even if we do discern the obstacles, it is to little avail since those obstacles appear to be impassable.

So there is a choice to be made, a choice that is freely available to anyone who seeks to take seriously a calling to Christian leadership. You can lay the foundation by cultivating your relationship with God, making it top priority in your life or you may choose to relegate the relationship to a lesser position. Appreciate, though, that choosing the former is a prerequisite for successful Christian leadership.

How does one make that choice—and really follow through on it? Let me first say how this is not done, because many have been sidetracked into this dead-end. It is not done by becoming more religious or by doing a lot of religious things. Relationship with God is different from religiosity. One leader in this study made this point so compellably that it deserves extended quotation. Jeff Pohlman, owner of Alpha Capital in Texas, wrote:

> It took awhile to learn this. In short, God let me know that I had "religion" down pat. However, I had little or no "relationship" with Him. Yes, I knew how to "pray," and I could be eloquent, covering all the bases of request with a heartfelt attitude. I knew how to "read the Word" and even dabble in Greek and Hebrew. I knew how to "give tithes and offerings." I knew how to "attend meetings" with fervency and regularity. I knew how to participate in "missions" and "local outreach programs." And I knew how to "evangelize." I was a "good person," and a doer at that. But, the Lord stopped me in my tracks and said that all I had amassed was a great ability to be religious. Those are all good things, not to be derided, but I had them out of order. They are to come after getting one thing straight. It was time to know Him first and deeply.

That quote speaks volumes because it shows that even seasoned Christians often buy-in to the myth that doing religious things is a pathway to growth. It's not a pathway, as many like this leader have learned through laborious and often painful trial-and-error. Instead, the pathway entails making the time to practice the spiritual disciplines taught by the giants of the faith for centuries, disciplines perhaps best summarized in the

To have something to give to other people, you need to be receiving as well. Be strong in the spiritual disciplines.

Keith Simila
Director of Engineering and
Aviation Management
USDA Forest Service
Alaska District

contemporary classic, *Celebration of Discipline*.[1] As shown there and in other fine resources on the subject,[2] the pathway entails spending time with God in prayer, worship, meditation and Bible study. It entails confessing sin, submitting to God's will and receiving encouragement and guidance from those who are more mature in the faith. It entails living a life of relative simplicity, making time for solitude, celebrating and enjoying life and cheerfully serving others. These are not legalistic requirements, more things for the to-do list. Rather, they collectively represent a lifestyle that puts us in a place where God generously pours out His grace. Many are familiar with the disciplines, but if you are not, know that they are the starting point for you. To become a better leader and a better Christian generally, become a student and a practitioner of the spiritual disciplines.

This is not new information. It is very old information. But it is timeless and among the most valuable information one can receive. Christlike leadership does not begin with a leadership book, with a sermon, with a course or with the knowledge of best practices and clever ideas. Such things are important adjuncts, but recognize that they are only adjuncts. Instead, Christlike leadership begins with Christ.

Notes

1. Foster, Richard J. *Celebration of Discipline: The Path to Spiritual Growth*, Harper: New York, 1978.
2. See, for example, *The Spirit of the Disciplines* and *The Divine Conspiracy* by Dallas Willard, *The Life You've Always Wanted* by John Ortberg and *Spiritual Disciplines for the Christian Life* by Donald Whitney.

CHAPTER 9

AN EXECUTIVE SUMMARY

In the preceding chapters, I have detailed the results of my study of Christian leaders and managers. For your convenience, this chapter serves as an executive summary, reviewing, in broad strokes, some of the intriguing things learned about Christian leadership through this project.

Employee Management

With regard to employee management, there is a primary tension facing every Christian leader: the balance between concern for employees and concern for production. That is, a balance between serving employees and enhancing organizational performance, between meeting people's needs and getting the job done more efficiently and effectively. Often there is overlap in these concerns and we are able to satisfy all needs simultaneously. Many best practices reside in this intersection. Other times, though, Christian leaders have to choose between competing concerns, and many permit concerns for performance to dominate concerns for employee needs.

Financial Stewardship

Christian leaders can follow prophets or chase profits. But the best ones find a way to do both, conceptualizing themselves as stewards of the financial resources placed at their disposal. I found here that leaders who are more stewardship-oriented in their beliefs also administer finances somewhat differently from their peers. They are more likely to pay all work-related bills on time, to stay within their budgets and to treat profit as a means, not an end. However, leaders in top management positions may find the faithful implementation of stewardship to be more challenging given the unique obstacles they face.

Business Acumen

Christian leaders are very confident in their abilities to serve the customer, to get results and to solve problems. They report being good planners with decent long-term vision, but admit significant room for improvement in their personal demeanor as they pursue their managerial objectives.

Unconventional Management Tools

Christian leaders view both Scripture and prayer as useful management tools. Those who do habitually seek God's will through prayer in the workplace experience tremendous blessings in both their leadership competence and their Christian character.

Witnessing in the Workplace

Evangelizing is a priority for some committed Christians but not others. Among those who do verbally witness at work, there is a lot of diversity in the frequency with which they choose to share the Gospel message.

Overall, it seems that those who verbally witness at work the most are those for whom witnessing is the natural outgrowth of a mature and growing relationship with God.

Model Christian Leadership

When God is working within a Christian, that person shows signs of God's supernatural presence. Commonly called "the fruit of the Spirit," leaders who report the greatest manifestation of these nine virtues have a distinct set of priorities and practices in the workplace with respect to employees, finances, customers and other stakeholders.

Primary Obstacles to Christlike Leadership

There are many stumbling blocks to a leader's successful implementation of Christian principles. My interviews with over 150 leaders put pride-related issues at the top, but identified several other obstinate barriers as well, including many entailing problems with communication.

The Secret to Better Christian Leadership

How does one overcome the major obstacles to be a more authentic, faithful Christian leader? A good start for many would be to temporarily shelve the leadership resources and instead, invest more time cultivating a closer relationship with God.

APPENDIX

THE METHODOLOGY FOR THIS STUDY

Design & Validity of the Survey Instrument

The data for this research come from the eighty-eight-item Regent University Christian Business Practices Study, designed in 1999–2000 and administered in the summer of 2000. It has seven sections, three of which are quantitative (Employee Management Issues and Other Business Issues, How Others View You at Work, Theological Perspectives), three of which are qualitative (Your Advice to Other Christians, People You Have Influenced On the Job, Your Definition of Servant Leadership) and one that is a combination (Demographic Information).

Each item in the survey is mapped to scripture, in particular, to the "Book of Proverbs," the Matthean Beatitudes (Matthew 5:3–12) and to Paul's "fruit of the Spirit" list in Galatians 5. To do this, I made significant use of my previous work, *Management by Proverbs*, and a colleague's work, *Be a Manager for God's Sake* (Bruce Winston, 1999), to generate the specific items. Thus, I ask in Item 1 about a leader's approachability because the exegesis in these resources concludes that Christian leaders should be approachable. Similarly, I ask about treating financial resources as God's resources, paying bills on time, the frequency of praising employees, etc., because such questions flow from these previously published works in applied Christianity. I ask about the "fruit of the Spirit" manifestations because this list is widely recognized as a succinct, if not exhaustive, enumeration of Christian character traits.

A panel of business professors at Regent University screened the initial set of survey items for clarity and content, making several useful recommendations and corrections. The survey was edited accordingly, reviewed again by the panel, re-edited, etc., until it achieved its final form, several iterations later. The expertise of many Christian scholars stands behind the subject matter and wording of this instrument.

Regarding scaling, for almost every item on the survey, I chose a six-point scale with relatively equidistant points: (1) Strongly disagree, (2) Moderately disagree, (3) Mildly disagree, (4) Mildly agree, (5) Moderately agree, and (6) Strongly agree. Note that there is no neutral middle point as in some other surveys. The rationale for offering no middle point is that Christian leaders who take the time to complete a long survey likely have some leaning on each issue raised in the survey. By compelling respondents to at least mildly agree or disagree with each item, I eliminated the possibility of respondents relying on a neutral middle point because of intellectual fatigue or laziness when completing the survey.

There are four other design strategies I employed to increase the validity of the data. First, there is a prominent caution at the beginning of the survey that says:

PLEASE READ THIS FIRST

The information that you provide on this survey is CONFIDENTIAL so please be candid in your responses. To do sound research, we need you to share with us your <u>actual</u> workplace attitudes and behaviors, rather than the attitudes and behaviors that you think should be reflected in a Christian manager. Thank you for taking the time to participate in what may prove to be a landmark study.

Second, items are worded to ensure that the "socially desirable" response is not always to agree with the statement. The rationale here is to minimize any sequencing bias—the tendency to keep circling, say, 5s, all the way down a column to just get through the survey expediently. An example is the following juxtaposition of items:

2. I consider it to be part of my job to quickly resolve conflicts among my employees

3. It is *not* my responsibility to reduce the work-related stress level of my employees

Third, some narrative items are worded to legitimize both agreement and disagreement with the statement, hence reducing the social desirability of either end of the spectrum. An example of this technique would be:

Some managers regularly seek input from their employees. Others find that decisions are made more smoothly when employees have little or no input. About how often do you seek input from your employees for the decisions you have to make (whether by one-on-one conversation, group meetings, email, phone or any other means)?

Fourth, we pilot-tested the survey with many of our Executive MBA students and friends of the faculty to fine-tune questions for clarity.

The Sample

I compiled the primary mailing list for this survey by (1) accessing the many Christian business directories freely available on the Internet and (2) identifying managers and leaders in the Regent University alumni and business student databases. I made a significant effort to balance the sample geographically (within the United States). The database drawn from the Internet included 1,201 names and addresses and the Regent database included 750 names and addresses. In total, I sent out 1,951 surveys.

Of the 1,951 surveys distributed, ninety-eight came back because of an outdated or inaccurate address. Twenty-seven of these were re-sent with corrected addresses, bringing the total distribution to 1,880 surveys. Of these, 328 were returned for a response rate of 17.4 percent. This response rate is somewhat low, but respectable given the length of the survey and the fact that this is essentially a "cold-calling" technique.

Because our mailing list is comprised exclusively of Christians who are (1) willing to list themselves as Christian leaders or managers in business directories, (2) affiliated with Christian-business organizations, or (3) current or former attendees of a Christian business school, my sample is likely more faith-centered and theologically conservative than marketplace Christians generally. However, in this study I am not trying to generalize about what "Christians" do at work. Rather, this exploratory research is limited to questions of the attitudes, priorities and practices of leaders who seek to apply their Christian faith in the workplace.

Data Analysis

Few of the conclusions in this study are based on the generation and examination of mere summary statistics like averages, standard deviations and frequencies. Although many of the tables and figures in this book may make the analysis look deceptively simplistic, in almost all cases the data were scrutinized through hypothesis tests, correlation analysis, multiple regressions, factor analysis and/or other relatively sophisticated techniques. Although the specifics of each analysis in this study are beyond the scope of this appendix, further information about any analysis, as well as some academic articles on selected subjects herein, are available from the author.

About the Author

Michael Zigarelli used to be a typical business professor, teaching, consulting, and publishing in mainstream areas of management and law. However, after many years of conducting traditional business research at Fairfield University (Connecticut), he sought to do something with his professional life that he considered to be more meaningful, more God-honoring: he chose to explore how the Christian faith applies to work and business.

As part of that transformation, he returned to graduate school to complete several seminary classes at Yale Divinity School, he began to write books on workplace Christianity and he accepted a teaching position at the Regent University Graduate School of Business, a leading Christian graduate school in Virginia.

This project, Ordinary People, Extraordinary Leaders, is the latest fruit of Dr. Zigarelli's renovated career, a rare application of scientific methodology to the issue of business from a Christian perspective. Dr. Zigarelli invites your comments on this work and can be reached by email at michzig@regent.edu.

REGENT UNIVERSITY
GRADUATE SCHOOL OF BUSINESS

Regent University's Graduate School of Business (RGSB) is dedicated to training men and women who will bring positive change to the global marketplace through their Christian integrity and professionalism. MBA graduates like Andrew Root, Deputy Director of U.S. Equity Research at Goldman Sachs; Susan Richmond, senior assistant and deputy White House liaison for Attorney General John Ashcroft; and Andrew Waites, CEO of eValueville, the largest clothing auction site on eBay are bringing excellence, innovation, and integrity into positions of influence.

RGSB is also dedicated to becoming a leading center of Christian thought and action. Business faculty are conducting research and publishing the results in academic journals and the popular press, writing books, conducting seminars for business leaders, and consulting with a variety of organizations.

RGSB is one of seven graduate schools housed on Regent University's main campus in Virginia Beach, Virginia. The others are government, law, education, communication, psychology and counseling, and divinity. The University also includes a center for leadership studies and a bachelor's degree completion program. In addition to the main campus, students may study near the nation's capital, at the Northern Virginia Graduate Center in Alexandria, or take courses online via Regent's Worldwide Campus. More than 2,800 students are enrolled in 28 graduate degree programs and the bachelor's program on the two campuses and online.